TECHIES UNITE!

FEATURING HELEN, SWEETHEART OF THE INTERNET

by

PETER E. ZALE

McGraw-Hill

NEW YORK   SAN FRANCISCO   WASHINGTON, D.C.
AUCKLAND   BOGOTÁ   CARACAS   LISBON   LONDON
MADRID   MEXICO CITY   MILAN   MONTREAL   NEW DELHI
SAN JUAN   SINGAPORE   SYDNEY   TOKYO   TORONTO

Library of Congress Cataloging-in-Publication Data applied for.

McGraw-Hill
A Division of The McGraw-Hill Companies

1 2 3 4 5 6 7 8 9 0   DOC/DOC   0 9 8 7 6 5 4 3 2 1 0

ISBN 0-07-136073-5

The designer was Michael Mendelsohn. Printed and bound by R. R. Donnelley & Sons Company.

Cover Illustration by Peter Zale; inking and coloring by Aaron McClellan.

McGraw-Hill books are available at special quantity discounts to use as premiums and sales promotions, or for use in corporate training programs. For more information, please write to the Director of Special Sales, Professional Publishing, McGraw-Hill, Two Penn Plaza, New York, NY 10121-2298. Or contact your local bookstore.

This book is dedicated to the women that give Helen life:
my wife Penelope Christo-Zale
and my daughters Elizabeth and Charlotte.
It's also dedicated to the women whose example inspired me:
my mother Jane Roberts, my aunt Pat Roberts Merena,
and my wise friend Mary Jane Shoultz.

ACKNOWLEDGMENTS

Besides Michelle Reed, a talented McGraw-Hill editor who initiated this whole shebang, I'd like to thank Ben Henick, who designed the Helen website (www.peterzale.com); Charley (Argon Zark) Parker, who roused the faithful; Bill Weinman, Lee Harrington, and Bill Shupp for hosting Helen at webmonster.net; my agent David Hendin for his counsel and friendship; Mike Peters for being my first friend in the business; Mike Fry for searching me out; Amy Lago for her invaluable help; Chris Baldwin for same; John Klossner for being brilliant; Jay Fife for same; Stuart Rees for knowing his job; Aaron McClellan for being there; John Miller, Marilyn Singer, Teddi Depner, Kate Evans, Tom Downing, and Craig Menefee for their critical acumen; Phyllis Li Rostykus for being Helen's older sister; the staff of Saifman, Richards & Associates for putting up with me; Jane Reynolds for taking a chance on an unknown; Fred Schecker, Eve Becker, and Mary Fischer for taking an even bigger chance; George and Rita Mouzoura for their support; Charles Schulz for caring; Garry Trudeau for setting my standard; and my brother Cooper JC Zale for starting all the stories.

Oh, yes, and you, too, Dad.

PETE

CONTENTS

FOREWORD

I have known Peter Zale for most of his life. We met when he was just a kid in Dayton, Ohio. He would come to the Dayton Daily News to show me his cartoons. It was obvious from the start that Peter was something special.

What amazed me most was his ability to create believable dialogue. He would capture personalities on paper which is hard at any age but nearly impossible for a young person. He had almost perfect pitch for character development.

Peter lived on Doonesbury and as we all know Doonesbury is all about character. But for a kid to know and love such a complex comic strip was phenomenal. And Peter created strips. He was prolific with characters. The next step of getting syndicated was of course more difficult.

When Peter was ready to become a professional cartoonist, he was able to avoid the fatal flaw of many would-be cartoonists. Most people who try to develop a strip fall in love with the concept or the characters. If the idea is not accepted they are crushed and discouraged. Peter was so prolific that as he was stuffing the envelope for a syndicated try, he was already thinking up a new comic strip. It was only a matter of time before his talent and his concepts met the perfect strip. But, of course, Peter would not settle for ordinary newspapers. He jumped to the Internet. Peter is one of the pioneers of Internet cartooning.

"Helen, Sweetheart of the Internet" is truly a strip for the 21st century. It meets all criteria for what will save our society. Peter has always been a philosopher as well as a writer and a cartoonist. In his strip we find a female hero who confronts the future and conquers it. He writes about relationships and people and real life. Peter Zale and his Helen will lead cartoons into the new world.

MIKE PETERS

ARTIFICIAL INTELLIGENCE

What do we do when our machines start talking back to us? With better English than we use? I think we accept the fact that these are our children and we've afforded them a better education than we got. We really ought to be proud.

In this chapter, Helen and her friends deal with a few different types of thinking machines, including talking assembly-line robots that wear nice suits; cars that prefer good driving music; and finally, software programs that, well, love people, and take care of them, whether they want it or not.

But to Helen, Artificial Intelligence is truly no different from the real kind, because next to her own, the existence of any intelligence is hardly noticeable.

SYLVIA, YOU FOUND THE PROBLEM WITH THE NETWORK?

YES. IT'S A VIRUS.

A VIRUS?

YES, BUT **VERY** CLOSE TO AN ARTIFICIAL INTELLIGENCE, LIKE ME.

HE'S **AMAZING**! HE TOOK OVER 13% OF THE COMPANY NETWORK JUST BY **WINKING** AT IT!

WINKING AT IT?

ARE YOU SAYING THIS THING IS **SEDUCING** MY SERVERS?!

HONEY, TRY TO UNDERSTAND... HE SPEAKS **EVERY** FLAVOR OF UNIX!

I'M AFRAID 15% OF OUR WORLD WIDE NETWORK HAS BEEN LOST TO THIS ROGUE VIRUS, HELEN. WE'LL HAVE TO SHUT DOWN.

BUT IT'LL TAKE **MONTHS** TO REBUILD THAT DATA!

CUT YOUR LOSSES, HON. EVEN NOW THE VIRUS IS TRYING TO REACH PAST YOUR FIREWALL!

CAN YOU SEE HIM?

HMM... YES I CAN...

WOW! CHECK OUT THOSE HUNKY **DATA STREAMS**!

OKAY! OKAY! SHUT DOWN!

THE KILLER VIRUS HAS BEEN PURGED, HELEN. THE SYSTEM IS SAFE.

FINALLY! SIGH...

THAT THING WAS INCREDIBLE! WHO COULD'VE CREATED SOMETHING LIKE THAT?

HARD TO SAY. BUT BEFORE IT DIED, I THINK I TRACED ITS ORIGIN TO GREEN BAY, WISCONSIN.

GREEN BAY, WISCONSIN? WHAT'S THERE?

WHAT INDEED!

YOU STILL TRYIN' TO IMPRESS THAT HELEN CHICK BY LEARNIN' PROGRAMMING, BOBBY?

YEAH, BUT I THINK I REALLY SCREWED SOMETHING UP!

IMAGE CASTING

Sybil had it easy.

All of us on the Web deal with constant put-ons... images cast out to entertain and attract us. These can come from sources as varied as political candidates or your friends next door. We're all vying for attention, and the best way to do that is to try to manufacture a face we think someone else wants to see.

Web sites, Web personas, Web identities change very rapidly because a) the first rule of the Web is fresh content, and b) the first rule of aging is that your own content doesn't stay fresh. Thus, in a nutshell, the Web changes 'cause we don't, and we freshen its content, because it's a whole lot easier than freshening ourselves.

This is a tough chapter for Helen because dealing with the fake faces people give is hard for her. Helen doesn't wear masks, and she finds it frustrating to understand people who do, people such as the marketing expert who has no idea what e-commerce is, or the classroom full of kids who think base 2 is where you want to get on a first date, or the boyfriend who won't notice your great emotional pain, but will notice your pager is missing.

Multiple personalities may be a disorder, but on the Web they're the order of business.

HELLO, BOYS AND GIRLS. MY NAME IS HELEN NICHOLS. SARAH POTTS ASKED ME TO COME IN TODAY TO GIVE ALL OF YOU A LITTLE TALK ON COMPUTERS.

NOW, WHILE ALL OF YOU HAVE USED COMPUTERS, YOU PROBABLY DON'T UNDERSTAND THE BASICS OF HOW THEY WORK...

FOR INSTANCE... DO ANY OF YOU KNOW WHAT BASE TWO IS?

I KNOW! I KNOW!

HAND UNDER THE BLOUSE, RIGHT?

UHH...

SO TO SUM UP... A CAREER IN HIGH TECHNOLOGY CAN WORK EQUALLY WELL FOR BOTH BOYS AND GIRLS!

UH, MS. NICHOLS, ARE YOU, UH, MARRIED?

NO.

DO YOU HAVE A BOYFRIEND?

UH, NO.

NO KIDDING. HEH HEH HEH...

TOMMY, STOP IT!

YEAH, YOU MEAT HEAD! DON'T BE SO INSENSITIVE!

I MEAN SHE PROBABLY FEELS BAD ENOUGH NOT HAVING ANY GOOD CLOTHES!

HELEN, HOW COME YOU DIDN'T GO TO SILICON VALLEY AND GET RICH?

'CAUSE IT'S ALL ABOUT TECHNOLOGY THERE, NOT PEOPLE.

SURE I COULD'VE GOTTEN RICH, BUT I WOULDN'T BE THE WARM, COMPASSIONATE PERSON I AM NOW!

NOW **THAT'S** A SCARY THOUGHT.

I KNOW! TO THINK WE MIGHT'VE MISSED THIS CLOSENESS!

HULLO, HELEN.

WHA- WHO ARE YOU?

I'M YOUR FANTASY. A MAN WHO LOOKS LIKE PIERCE BROSNAN AND THINKS LIKE ALBERT EINSTEIN.

OH, MY GOD!

AND I... I...

...AM SO SORRY. I HAVE TO GO SAVE THE WORLD.

I HATE MY FANTASY LIFE.

...AND WE UPDATE OUR **EXTRANET** DAILY WITH JOB EXPENSES FOR OUR CLIENTS.

HMM...

WHAT SORT OF **RDBM** SYSTEM YOU GOT?

A CUTE LITTLE THING WITH SOME FRONT-END SCRIPT YOU'LL LIKE.

HEY, THAT'S MY CODE!

I KNOW! I FOUND IT ON THE WEB.

GOLLY... I WROTE THAT WHEN I WAS 14!

SO **THAT'S** WHY MATT DILLON'S FACE KEEPS APPEARING ON THE RIGHT THERE!

I SWEAR, HELEN... I WILL SEE YOU **FIRED** FROM MARTIN-KIRBY!

YOUR MUSTACHE TWITCHES WHEN YOU GET MAD, MR. CFO.

YOU'RE OUT OF CONTROL! YOU'RE LIKE A RAMPANT VIRUS IN THIS CORPORATION!

A **COMPUTER** VIRUS?

ACTUALLY I WAS SPEAKING BIOLOGICALLY.

ARE YOU SURE I'M A VIRUS THEN, AND NOT SOME FORM OF STREP INFECTION?

WELL, NOW THAT YOU MENTION IT, THAT IS KIND OF A FASCINATING COMPARISON. I'VE ALWAYS THOUGHT...

THERE IS NO GEEK I CANNOT TAME.

HELEN, IT'S SUCH A DELIGHT TO SEE YOU AGAIN. IMAGINE RUNNING INTO A FAVORITE OLD STUDENT LIKE THIS!

WELL, I'M SO GLAD YOU HAD TIME FOR LUNCH, DAVID.

STILL READING THE BARD?

YES. IN FACT, I REREAD "ROMEO AND JULIET" LAST NIGHT.

MM.. SEEMS I REMEMBER YOUR FIRST READING OF "ROMEO AND JULIET" IN MY CLASS.

HEH HEH. I REMEMBER THAT MYSELF.

"O, SWEAR NOT BY THE MOON, TH' INCONSTANT MOON..."

UH, HELEN!

GWEN, DO YOU THINK I HAVE A BAD SELF-IMAGE?

YES.

THAT'S NOT WHAT I MEANT!

SPENCER, DO I HAVE A BAD SELF-IMAGE?

NO.

WAIT. DOES THAT MEAN I LIKE MYSELF OR I SIMPLY LOOK GOOD?

YOU LIKE YOURSELF.

OH.

WAIT. DOES THAT MEAN...

BETTER DRINK THIS QUICK.

23

UNITED AIRLINES FLIGHT #116...

HEY, AN E-MAIL FROM BOBBY TUCKER IN GREEN BAY! I SHOULD VISIT HIM.

OKAY... FLIGHT SCHEDULES. GOOD... AND... **THERE!**

CLICK!

UH, THIS IS THE CAPTAIN. WE'VE JUST BEEN, UM, INEXPLICABLY REROUTED TO, UH GREEN BAY, WISCONSIN.

I HOPE THEY HAVE AN AIRPORT.

I HOPE THEY HAVE AN AIRPORT.

WAIT! YOU CAN'T GO PAST HERE!

WHY NOT? BOBBY TUCKER INVITED ME!

PACKERS

YEAH, RIGHT. THE FINEST QUARTERBACK IN FOOTBALL INVITED SOME BLONDE BIMBO TO WATCH HIM PRACTICE!

WHA-?

WHAT DID YOU JUST CALL ME?

A BLONDE BIMBO.

THAT'S DEROGATORY!

DEROGATORY... DISHWATER... STRAWBERRY... IT'S **STILL** BLONDE!

GREEN BAY PACKER PRACTICE SESSION, 11:44 A.M.

LET ME IN! I WANT TO SEE BOBBY!

WHO IS THIS, JOE?

SAYS SHE'S A FRIEND OF OUR STAR QUARTER-BACK.

LET HER IN. THE WAY BOBBY LOOKED AGAINST DALLAS, HE COULD USE THE HELP!

IS BOBBY ILL?

NAH. HE'S JUST NOT THROWIN' THE BALL WELL.

IT'S ALL AERODYNAMICS.

NAH, THEY'VE BEEN BANNED.

VOYEURISM

Think about it... Isn't the Web totally voyeuristic? The very idea of a virtual self is voyeurism to the core. You're there but you're not. You watch, but you don't participate. You exist but you don't...

Certainly many that present themselves on the Web have no notion of any "real" audience. How else can you explain naked exhibitionism by amateurs and pictures of polka parties? I mean this gets a little much.

Surreptitiously, we peek into Helen's life in this chapter, at her attempts at love, her dreams, and her fantasies. We see her aboard starships flirting with alien lizards and in nightclubs flirting with serpentine men. We see her in places she probably doesn't want to be seen in. Yet it is our right to do so because she really doesn't have any existence, virtual or otherwise, without our voyeurism.

PHIL, I HAVE TO TALK TO YOU ABOUT SOMETHING.

WHAT?

UM, ACCORDING TO MY RECORDS, YOU'VE BEEN SPENDING TIME AT AN "IMPOLITE" WEB SITE.

PAMELA LEE'S POLITE!

AND QUITE ACCOMMODATING I HEAR.

I FEEL ASHAMED FOR VISITING THAT PAMELA LEE WEB SITE.

DON'T, PHIL. THE WEB TEMPTS EVERYONE.

IN FACT, I'VE EVEN USED THE WEB TO FULFILL MY SECRET SHAMEFACED DESIRES!

SEE?

SEARS.COM?

THEY SELL UNMENTIONABLES!

WHAT IS IT, PHIL?

SOMETHING'S WRONG WITH HELEN.

LATELY SHE SEEMS... I DON'T KNOW.

COLD?

YEAH! REALLY COLD! USED TO BE YOU COULD FEEL WARMTH BEATING RIGHT UNDER THE SURFACE...

IN HER OR YOU?

I'D SAY YOU'VE CHANGED, TOO.

YOU GUYS'RE RIGHT! I'VE BEEN **BLIND**!

THE INTERNET IS **EVERYTHING**! TECHNOLOGY IS **HOPE**! THAT'S WHAT I'M ALL ABOUT! THAT'S WHAT MATTERS!

MY SPEECH HAS LEFT YOU DUMBFOUNDED WITH EXCITEMENT, HUH?

HER SECOND BUTTON CAME UNBUTTONED!

HI, DOUG. I SEE YOU'RE WORKING HARD.

YEAH. REPORT TO GET OUT.

YOU KNOW, I'VE BEEN THINKING... REMEMBER ALL THOSE NASTY THINGS I SAID ABOUT YOU?

YES.

AND THOSE AWFUL JOKES I PLAYED?

YEAH.

WOW! YOU HAVE MORE BRAIN CAPACITY THAN I THOUGHT!

I SEE HELEN'S STILL IN A KILLING MOOD.

YEAH.

SHE'S **HACKING** INTO OTHER COMPANIES' SITES AND MESSING WITH THEM.

THAT'S HOW SHE DEALS WITH STRESS.

ISN'T THAT **DANGEROUS**, THOUGH? WON'T THE LAW TRACK HER DOWN?

MY GUESS IS HELEN HAS **REDIRECTED** ANY SEARCH THEY MIGHT TRY...

WE MIGHT'VE **FIGURED** YOU'D BE A WHIZ AT THIS KIND OF ELECTRONIC SABOTAGE, TOO, LINDA TRIPP!

B-BUT...

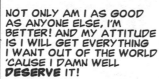

YOU SEEM INORDINATELY PENSIVE TODAY, HELEN. WHAT'S WRONG?

SIGH...

I'M, UH... GOING TO BE 24 TOMORROW.

OH, YOUR BIRTHDAY, THAT'S RIGHT. CLONING'S ILLEGAL.

SPENCER, I HAVE A VISION FOR US OF A COMPLETELY HEALTHY LIFESTYLE!

LIKE A PHYSICS EQUATION, IF WE INPUT THE RIGHT ENERGY, OUR LIFE-RATE OUTPUT SHOULD BE EXCELLENT.

HENCE, I'VE PUT TOGETHER A COMPREHENSIVE FOOD AND LIQUID INTAKE PLAN TO COVER THE NEXT 65+ YEARS.

WHAT DO YOU THINK?

I WANT TO START SMOKING.

HOW COULD YOU START SMOKING?!

BECAUSE OF THE **SUCCESS** OF OUR RELATIONSHIP, HELEN.

AS IN CLASSIC OLD MOVIES, LIKE "CASABLANCA," SMOKING CIGARETTES CONFIRMS THE ROMANTIC CHEMISTRY BETWEEN A MAN AND A WOMAN.

IN FACT, THE TYPE OF CIGARETTE SMOKED BEARS ON THE **INTENSITY** OF THAT ROMANTIC CHEMISTRY.

AND WHAT DO YOU WANT TO SMOKE?

CAMEL STRAIGHTS. NO FILTER, BABY!

YOU'RE JUST SAYING THAT.

TECHIES UNITE!

But with Helen and Spencer, it always ends like this...

HOW COULD YOU CHEAT ON ME, SPENCER?!

HELEN, IT WAS INEVITABLE!

WE'RE FRIENDS, NOT LOVERS! OPENING UP TO EACH OTHER AND SHARING INTIMATELY IS THE **LAST** THING EITHER ONE OF US WANTS!

YEAH. **NOW!**

OKAY.

HELEN...

OH, MELISSA... I'M SO EMBARRASSED!

BUT **WHY?**

I'VE BEEN CRYING FOR **THREE DAYS!** THAT'S WHY!

THAT LOUSY CRUMB SPENCER HAS TURNED ME INTO A WEEPY, UNCONTROLLED **FOOL!**

I DIDN'T THINK HE HAD IT IN 'IM!

GOOD. STILL COMPETITIVE.

FOR REASONS ABOUT TO BECOME CLEAR, HELEN IS SPENDING A RESTLESS NIGHT ABOARD **BABYLON 5!**

SCOTCH ON THE ROCKS.

EVIAN WATER PLEASE.

SO, IS IT GETTING ANY BETTER?

NOT REALLY, MICHAEL. IM STILL DEPRESSED. STILL BASICALLY OFF MY ROCKER.

YKNOW. FOR A GORGEOUS GENIUS YOU GOT **ZIPPO** SELF-ESTEEM!

PART OF THE PACKAGE! THATS WHY I GO NUTS EVERY TIME SPENCER DUMPS ME.

SO THIS **BABYLON 5** DREAM IS TO WORK OUT DEEP-SEATED PROBLEMS YOU HAVE?

NO, BELIEVE IT OR NOT, ITS AN UNDIGESTED BIT OF BEEF.

HELEN DREAMS SHE IS ABOARD BABYLON 5!

CAPTAIN SHERIDAN, I'M JUST NOT MYSELF. I'M NOT HAPPY.

YOU LOVE SPENCER THAT MUCH?

I GUESS. I DON'T KNOW. I... **SOB**...

IT'S ALL RIGHT.

I DON'T KNOW WHY I LET HIM **DO** THIS TO ME!

BECAUSE YOU'RE A WOMAN, AND WOMEN LIKE **MYSTERIOUS MEN!**

SIGH... DID THE **VORLONS** PROGRAM US THIS WAY?

NO. HOLLYWOOD.

HELEN'S BABYLON 5 DREAM CONTINUES!

I KNOW THIS IS A DREAM, HELEN, BUT YOU HAVE TO LISTEN TO IT.

I HAVE A CHOICE?

WHAT YOU WANT YOU CAN'T HAVE! YOU CAN'T RECLAIM YOUR INNOCENCE. YOU CAN'T GO BACK WHERE YOU STARTED.

WHY NOT?

BECAUSE LIFE DOESN'T WORK THAT WAY!

ONLY BECAUSE WE HAVEN'T FIGURED OUT HOW TO WARP TIME AND SPACE!

WELL, WHEN THAT HAPPENS, MAYBE YOU CAN GO BACK AND—

SHUT-UP, WINDBAG!

HELEN'S BABYLON 5 DREAM NEARS COMPLETION!

G'KAR, YOU'RE THE WISEST BEING ON BABYLON 5. CAN YOU TELL ME HOW I CAN FEEL LIKE I USED TO FEEL?

YOU MEAN OPTIMISTIC?

EXACTLY!

WELL, YOU COULD GO OUT ON A DATE WITH A SLIGHTLY REPTILIAN LOOKING ALIEN WITH FOREHEAD SPOTS.

THAT'LL CURE ME?

ABSOLUTELY!

OBVIOUSLY **YOU'RE** PRETTY OPTIMISTIC.

IT RUBS OFF.

37

THE VOID

There is a void. It is endless, aimless, shrouded in enigma and wrapped in mystery. There is a Sphinx staring at us and laughing at our feeble attempts to understand it and, worse, our attempts to use it for our benefit. There is a void, ladies and gentlemen, that is truly unknowable even with a darn good search engine.

Without a purpose and a focus, the Internet is just a mess o' information, staring back and overwhelming us with its size and utter meaninglessness. Without a reason to surf it, the Web swallows us. Helen though finds people like to be similar, since they are not possessed of the degree of motivation she counts on every day. Hence Helen can and does get lost in her feelings for the rest of us.

That is why, ultimately, Helen commands her friends so stringently. She really can't fathom their relationship to her. She can only push herself through to a relationship objective she understands, one that rarely includes the goal of actually having a relationship.

WHAT'S THE MATTER, HELEN?

I'VE BEEN SURFING THE WEB TOO LONG, LUCY.

IT'S LIKE LOOKING AT THE STARS AND CONTEMPLATING THE ABYSS.

WITH BANNER ADS.

HELEN, DO YOU THINK THE INTERNET GETS US CLOSER TO GOD?

WHAT?

IF GOD IS IN ALL OF US, DOESN'T CONNECTING US PUT GOD TOGETHER?

ARE YOU SAYING GOD'S AN OPEN SOURCE PROGRAM?

WELL, I AM A UNITARIAN.

LUCY, I DON'T KNOW WHAT THE INTERNET MEANS TO US SPIRITUALLY. I JUST KNOW IT'S A MEANS TO AN END.

WHAT END?

WELL, INTERFACING WITH PEOPLE...

EXACTLY! AND EVENTUALLY EVERYONE ON THE PLANET WILL BE DOING IT AT THE SAME TIME!

THAT HAS TO MEAN SOMETHING!

HELLACIOUS BANDWIDTH ISSUES?

41

HOW LONG HAVE YOU WORKED IN COMPUTERS, MAGGIE?

JUST A FEW YEARS, REALLY...

I'M A GRAPHIC DESIGNER BY TRADE. I JUST GOT INVOLVED IN HI-TECH BASICALLY TO KEEP UP IN MY OWN FIELD.

THEN OF COURSE MY COMPANY KICKED ME UPSTAIRS. EVENTUALLY I KNEW SO MUCH I HAD TO GET THE CEO AND THE PRESIDENT OF THE FIRM FIRED BECAUSE THEY SIMPLY COULDN'T ADAPT TO HOW I HAD EVOLVED THE SYSTEMS.

YOU KNOW, I CAN'T TELL YOU HOW MANY OF MY FRIENDS HAVE HAD TO DO THAT!

WELL, AS USUAL, HELEN, YOU'RE GETTING ALL THE STARES.

EXCUSE ME. I THINK I KNOW YOU.

THAT WOULD BE INTRIGUING. WHO ARE YOU?

I'M MIKE. I RUN MY OWN START-UP COMPANY CALLED "OMNI TECH."

OH, YEAH! YOU'RE THAT MID-LEVEL PROGRAMMER I FIRED LAST APRIL! SO, HOW'S THE NEW VENTURE?

ULP... WELL, SPEAKING AT THIS PARTICULAR INSTANT, RATHER DEAD IN THE WATER.

YEAH, YOU SUCKED WHEN YOU WORKED FOR ME, TOO.

WHAT ARE YOU LOOKING AT, LUCY?

IT'S A MEDICAL SITE.

YOU TYPE IN YOUR SYMPTOMS AND IT GIVES A DIAGNOSIS.

WHAT ARE YOUR SYMPTOMS?

STRESS, TERROR, DEMENTIA AND LACK OF SLEEP.

DIAGNOSIS: YOU'RE ALIVE.

"DIAGNOSIS: YOU WORK FOR HELEN."

EVENTUALLY, SPENCER, THE INTERNET WILL LET US SHOP, VOTE, AND WORK WITHOUT GOING TO A STORE, SCHOOL OR OFFICE. IT WILL MAKE LIFE INCREDIBLY EASIER.

BUT WAIT, HELEN...

AREN'T PEOPLE ISOLATED FROM EACH OTHER TO A DEADLY DEGREE ALREADY? WHY DO WE NEED THE INTERNET TO DO IT EVEN MORE?

PROGRESS?

THIS THING **WAS** DESIGNED FOR NUCLEAR WAR, **WASN'T** IT?

WHAT KIND OF COMPUTER DO YOU HAVE, HELEN?

COMPUTER**S**, SPENCER.

I HAVE A UNIX SYSTEM, A PENTIUM RUNNING WINDOWS, AND A MACINTOSH.

MY MAC IS MY FAVORITE! BUT – SHHH! – DON'T TELL MY OTHER COMPUTERS THAT!

PERHAPS YOU SHOULDN'T TELL ANY OTHER HUMANS EITHER.

DO YOU SPEND A LOT OF TIME WITH YOUR COMPUTERS, HELEN?

NO MORE THAN MOST PEOPLE. 16 TO 19 HOURS A DAY.

YOU DON'T GET LONELY?

NO. NOT REALLY.

MMFF!

I WAS THINKING OF GETTING A CAT.

POWER

Is it just me, or does everyone understand the connection between power and innocence? Certainly any parent of a newborn does. Isn't innocence what we worship? Like God above us? All seeing, all knowing, all... innocent?

Heavy. And so is Helen in her way, resting atop us in the ego food chain, dishing out orders and truth with godlike authenticity. "Godlike?" you say? Why not? We ascribe to the supernatural that which we cannot understand, and can you understand routers? Why shouldn't Helen occupy a spot higher than humanity? After all, she assigns the passwords.

But being worshipped isn't always what it's cracked up to be. It's a great responsibility for one thing, a responsibility Helen can handle only because she is a true innocent and therefore impervious to moral and ethical dilemmas. As the strips in this chapter show, her use of power at work, at play, and in attack is as pure and unfettered as the first A-Bomb. "Look, ma! I just blew up Los Alamos!"

I'M SO IMPRESSED, MAGGIE! HERE YOU ARE... I.S. MANAGER OF A **HUGE** AD AGENCY!

WELL, I HOPE YOU FIND YOUR VISIT HERE AN EDUCATION, DEAR.

I'M SURE I'LL—

HEY, BILL! THE CLIENT CALLED. THE EPS FILE YOU MADE LOOKS CRUDDY ON HIS WINDOWS P.C.

EPS ONLY RESOLVES WELL ON A MAC, FRED. THE GUY NEEDS A WINDOWS METAFILE.

OH.

IT'S SO GREAT YOU ENCOURAGE YOUR CHILDREN TO USE THEIR WORDS LIKE THAT.

WORKDAY: 8:37AM...

AND THIS IS WHO, HELEN?

SPENCER! MY MAN!

YOU MEAN YOUR BOYFRIEND?

I MEAN MY MAN! MY MATCH! MY CHOSEN! MY **MATE**!

OH.

WELL, IN THAT CASE, DOES HE NEED A W2?

HEY! WANT ONE?

HMMM...

WELL, HELEN, IT WAS GREAT TO MEET SPENCER, BUT WE DO HAVE AN EARLY MEETING, SO...

UH-UH! WHERE I GO, **HE** GOES!

I DON'T WANT HIM OUT OF MY SIGHT!

UH...

WELL, OKAY, BUT I DON'T THINK YOU SHOULD GO—

EEEEEEE!!

SIGH... I GUESS THAT'LL PRIME THE PUMP FOR UNISEX BATHROOMS.

YOU NEVER TOLD ME WHY YOU QUIT, HELEN.

I WAS TIRED, PHIL.

WE ALL GET TIRED AND SAD AND END UP GRASPING FOR WHATEVER SHRED OF HOPE WE CAN FIND.

SO, ANYWAY, I JUST FIRED THE SHIPPING DEPARTMENT.

SO THEY CAN GRASP AT SHREDS, TOO?

HELEN. CALL ON LINE ONE.

HELLO.

COMPUTER PIRATE SILVER HERE.

OH, NO. BENNY, GET OFF THE LINE!

HEY, BUCCANEER! HOW'S IT GOING?

WHY ARE YOU CALLING ME?

'CAUSE I'M RELEASING A KILLER VIRUS, AND I DON'T WANT YOUR COMPUTERS TO CRASH!

MINE? CRASH?

HA HA HA...

ALL RIGHT. I DON'T WANT THEM TO BE SOMEWHAT **ANNOYED**.

PHIL, IS HELEN ALL RIGHT?

IS SHE GETTING EVEN MORE TYRANNICAL THAN USUAL?

NO! IN FACT, TODAY SHE'S ALL SWEETNESS AND LIGHT, WHICH FRANKLY IS SCARIER.

WHAT DO YOU MEAN?

SHE'S LEADING THE R & D DEPARTMENT IN A SING-A-LONG.

JAVA SCRIPT'S THE COOLEST THING! HALLELUUUUUJAH!

HELEN, YOU BLOCKED MY STAFF'S CONNECTION TO THE INTERNET!

THEY WERE DOWNLOADING PICTURES DEMEANING TO WOMEN, DOUG. I DID IT, AND I'D DO IT AGAIN!

DAMMIT, I WILL NOT BE SPOKEN TO THIS WAY BY YOU!

ACTUALLY YOU WON'T BE SPOKEN TO BY ME AT ALL. BYE.

HOW COME I CAN NEVER IMPRESS WOMEN LIKE THAT?

HELEN, I'M HEARING ALL SORTS OF THINGS ABOUT OUR WEBSITE CHANGING.

HEY... XML, DHTML, DATABLADES, FLASH.. CHANGE IS **CONSTANT** ON THE WEB, PHIL.

WELL, COULD I BE **INFORMED** OF THESE CHANGES?

THE LEARNING CURVE'S A BIT STEEP FOR YOU, KID. I WOULDN'T SWEAT IT.

HELEN, I AM YOUR SUPERVISOR.

AND YOU DO A **GREAT** JOB OF IT! NOW LEAVE ME ALONE. I'VE GOT WORK TO DO.

THE PROBLEM I HAVE IS I HAVE TO GO BACK TO SCHOOL FOR A YEAR TO FIGURE OUT WHEN SHE'S **DISSING** ME.

LOOK! HELEN'S BACK!

HEY!

ALLRIGHT!

GREAT TO HAVE YOU BACK!

PLACE WASN'T THE SAME!

YOU LOOK TERRIFIC!

YEAH!

SIGH...

OKAY, GO.

MY PC'S CRASHED!

MY LOGIC BOARD...

HOW DO YOU OPEN...

GUYS, THE SECRET TO WRITING GOOD PROGRAM CODE IS WHETHER IT WORKS FOR WHOM IT'S INTENDED.

GOBS OF NIFTY CODE IS FUN, BUT YOU HAVE TO CONSIDER THE CLIENT SYSTEM IT'S GOING TO RUN ON.

YOU CAN'T DO WHATEVER YOU WANT AND EXPECT YOUR ENTHUSIASM TO MAKE IT WORK.

BUT, WE WERE BROUGHT UP IN THE REAGAN YEARS!

YOU DONE WITH ALL THE UPGRADES, HELEN?

NOT QUITE, PHIL...

I'VE UPGRADED ALL THE MACHINES...

...BUT I STILL HAVE THIS TO...

CLICK!

OH MY GOD! I'VE BEEN FIRED!

NOW I'M DONE.

HEY, WHEN I GET TO THE MEETING, DO YOU THINK THE AIR TRAFFIC COUNCIL WILL TELL ME YOUR SOFTWARE'S A "SMASHING" SUCCESS?

HEE HEE HEE...

TAP
TAP
TAP
TAP
TAP
TAP
TAP
TAP
TAP
TAP!

?

DON'T TELL ME... YOU'VE REROUTED MY FLIGHT TO DAYTON THROUGH THE PHILIPPINES.

TWICE!

PHIL, YOU GOTTA STOP DOUG AND HIS CRONIES FROM BEING SO OBNOXIOUS!

THEY'RE MEN, HELEN. IT'S HOW THEY BLOW OFF STEAM.

IT'S NOT APPROPRIATE!

NEITHER WAS YOUR CAUSING ANYONE WHO ACCESSED A NON-BUSINESS WEB SITE TO GET AN ELECTRIC SHOCK!

I HAVE VERY LITTLE HAIR AS IT IS!

WHY ARE YOU TECHS SO CONSTANTLY ANNOYED?

YOU GUYS JUST DON'T GET IT...

WE'RE RUNNING THINGS! EVERY ONE OF YOUR JOBS DEPENDS ON WHETHER OR NOT WE CAN DO OURS!

AND YOU THINK WE WORK FOR YOU!

IT'S THE LONG HOURS, ISN'T IT?

LOOKING FORWARD TO THE STATE-OF-THE-COMPANY MEETING, HELEN?

LIKE A ROOT CANAL!

UH-HUH. I SEE YOU DRESSED.

RISQUÉ I MIGHT ADD. NOTE THE LOW CUT TENNIS SHOES.

YOU THINK MEETINGS ARE AN ABSOLUTE PAIN, DON'T YOU?

THEY WOULD NEED TO RISE SEVERAL LEVELS OF HELL TO BE JUST THAT!

WOOH! I THINK SOMEONE NEEDS AN ATTITUDE ADJUSTMENT.

I THINK I NEED A **PROSCRIPTION LIST!**

I'M TIRED OF FIGHTING, HELEN. LET'S CALL A TRUCE.

WHY?

I'VE BEATEN YOU SO UTTERLY IT'S NEVER RISEN TO THE LEVEL OF A FIGHT.

SO WHAT TRUCE IS THERE TO CALL?

IF YOU WANT TO CALL SOMETHING, CALL THE BATTERED VICTIMS SHELTER.

SO HOW WAS YOUR DAY, HELEN?

TERRIBLE! A MANAGERIAL NIGHTMARE!

RENEGADE PROGRAMMERS... BANDWIDTH HOGS... PEOPLE USING SOFTWARE THEY'RE NOT LICENSED FOR...

SIGH...

YOU KNOW, MUSSOLINI NEVER GOT THE CREDIT HE—

OOP! MY TRAIN!

I CAN'T BELIEVE YOU MADE THAT RUDE JOKE IN FRONT OF A CLIENT! SOMETIMES YOU MAKE ME SO MAD!

YEAH. YEAH.

BOOP BOOP BEEP BEEP!

WHAT NOW?

I KNOW! YOU'RE MAKING YOURSELF FEEL BETTER BY ORDERING FROM THE WEB ON YOUR CELL PHONE, AREN'T YOU?.

UH-HUH.

65

CONNECTIONS

The Web's a morass, a pit. It's pandemonium and chaos. It is Beelzebub's dream, a virtual hell, a lake of fire wire.

That said, it's a terrific place to get in touch with your friends.

In this chapter, we see Helen connecting; making ties with friends, with acquaintances and even enemies! We see her exposing that special, private side of herself that needs the closeness of others — at least until that new circuit board arrives in the mail and she can get back to work.

A word of warning: It is sometimes good to take connections with Helen in small doses. Her brain holds so much pure energy that only the power of her heart can keep it from atomizing you. But her patience is thin. Stay too long in her presence and you may get a glimpse of Heaven from the same ultimate perspective as Lucifer.

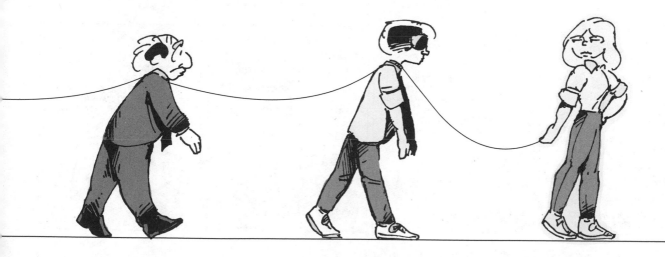

HELEN, WE'VE GOT AN INTERESTING NEW CLIENT.

WHO?

A COMPANY CALLED ROCKETECH. THEY WANT TO BE THE FIRST PRIVATE FIRM TO PUT A MAN IN SPACE.

I'M NOT GOING.

COME ON, DOUG! THINK OF IT AS BEING OUR **EXTREMELY** WESTERN MARKETING MANAGER!

ROCKETECH IS A PRIVATE COMPANY THAT WANTS TO INITIATE A SPACE PROGRAM?

YES. FOR TRIPS. VACATIONS. LIKE THAT.

AND WHAT ARE WE SUPPOSED TO DO?

COME UP WITH ENGINEERING MODELS FOR SATELLITE HOTELS, REFUELING STATIONS, ETC.

WOW. I GUESS UTOPIA'S FINALLY HERE.

OH, YES. AND A McDONALD'S.

UTOPIA WITH CHEESE.

IT'S FUNNY HOW BEING A GEEK IS SO FASHIONABLE THESE DAYS.

THAT'S 'CAUSE OF ALL THE MONEY THEY MAKE!

TRUE. BUT I THINK THERE'S ALSO SOMETHING TO THE "SEDENTARY" NATURE OF GEEKNESS THAT PEOPLE LIKE.

AS IF WE WERE EVOLVING TO ACCEPT HAVING FAT AND USELESS BODIES.

THAT WOULD EXPLAIN GOLF.

HELEN, I DON'T THINK I'VE EVER UNDERSTOOD THE GEEK MINDSET.

THAT'S 'CAUSE THERE ISN'T ONE!

"GEEK" IS A MADE UP TERM. IT'S MEANINGLESS!

NOT TRUE. IT MEANS "AWKWARD AND UGLY."

WELL, MAYBE NOT IN MY IMMEDIATE RADIUS.

I FEEL BAD, MAGGIE. I KNOW YOU HOPED SPENCER AND I WOULD BE MARRIED BY NOW.

IT'S ALL RIGHT, DEAR.

I JUST HOPED...

I JUST HOPED TO HAVE A DAUGHTER AS TECHNICALLY MINDED AS I WAS!

REALLY GEEKED ABOUT IT, WEREN'T YOU?

ON SO MANY LEVELS!

MAGGIE, EVEN IF SPENCER AND I NEVER MARRY, YOU AND I WILL ALWAYS BE FRIENDS!

I KNOW, DEAR...

BUT WITH HIM IN COMMON, WE HAD OUR TOUCHSTONE, OUR BRIDGE...

OUR MEANS TO TRANSCEND OUR AGE DIFFERENCE, OUR DIFFERENT PERSPECTIVES AND SPEEDS OF LOOKING AT THE WORLD!

HE WAS A GREAT ROUTER, WASN'T HE?

CISCO COULDN'T DO IT BETTER!

HELEN, DO WE "GET IT?"

COME AGAIN, PHIL.

WELL, I WAS READING WHERE SOME COMPANIES "GET" THE INTERNET, AND SOME DON'T.

OH, WE GET IT.

WE GOT IT...

AND THE COMPETITION'S GONNA *GET* IT!

PHIL, HELEN SAYS TECHIES ARE THE DEARTH OF WESTERN CIVILIZATION.

WELL, SHE WOULD KNOW.

NO. SHE DIDN'T MEAN HER.

WELL, I WOULD EXPECT THAT, TOO.

HMM...

WHO DO YOU THINK SHE MEANT?

WELL, AT THE MOMENT..!

HELEN, IT APPEARS TO ME THE HIGH-TECH REVOLUTION IS BEING LED BY CHILDREN.

WHAT REVOLUTION ISN'T?

WIRED

HOW GROWN UP COULD LENIN HAVE BEEN TO RABBLE ROUSE SO? OR MAO?

BELIEVE ME, THE MOST DANGEROUS RADICALS ARE ALL BASICALLY KIDS.

THAT'S QUITE AN INSIGHT.

BARBIE SAYS: "THANK YOU!"

BING!
"Have you considered the tremendous credit opportunities available..."

!

TAP
TAP
TAP
TAP
TAP
TAP
TAP
TAP
TAP'
TAP
TAP

TAP!

BING!
"We would like to apologize for our recent unsolicited e-mail advertisement. Our entire server network has bombed, and our social security numbers and tax records have all suddenly become public domain. As such, we have decided to cease and desist ever again bothering you very nice people.."

BULK E-MAIL IS SUCH A TIME WASTER.

ALL RIGHT, WHAT IS "CLIENT-SERVER TECHNOLOGY?"

WHY DO YOU WANT TO KNOW, JOHN?

WELL, I DO RUN THE COMPANY.

CLIENT-SERVER TECHNOLOGY ALLOWS A REMOTE USER TO ACCESS A SERVER AND WORK EASILY WITH THE DATA ON THAT SERVER.

OH. THAT DOESN'T SOUND LIKE SUCH A BIG DEAL.

IT ISN'T.

THEN HOW COME OUR STOCK KEEPS GOING THROUGH THE ROOF BECAUSE OF IT!?

THAT INVOLVES SOMETHING CALLED "GREEDY-SUCKER TECHNOLOGY..."

HELEN, I WANT OUR PEOPLE TO FUNCTION SMOOTHLY WITH OUR TECHNOLOGY!

RIGHT, JOHN.

WHAT STANDS IN THE WAY OF OUR DOING THAT?

THE FACT THAT YOU'VE ALL PROVEN YOURSELVES TO BE TECHNICALLY INCOMPETENT.

HUH?

WELL, EXCEPT PHIL...

TH-THEN WE'LL BUILD AROUND PHIL.

AND THAT'S BECAUSE PHIL NEVER TURNS ON HIS COMPUTER.

ANOTHER QUESTION FOR YOU, HELEN... WHAT IS THIS "S. Q. L." STUFF WE MENTION IN OUR ADS?

STRUCTURED QUERY LANGUAGE...

IT'S PROGRAMMING INVOLVED WITH CLIENT-SERVER TECHNOLOGY.

OH.

WELL, I'M TOTALLY CONFUSED...

BUT, DAMN, SINCE I RUN THE COMPANY, DON'T I SEEM SMART!

SIGH...CERTAINLY SMARTER THAN THE PEOPLE WHO WORK FOR YOU, JOHN.

THANK, GOD, HELEN. WHERE HAVE YOU BEEN?

TAKING A LONG LUNCH. WHAT'S GOING ON?

THE SERVER ROUTER ISN'T WORKING, AND EVERYONE'S BLAMING EVERYONE ELSE.

GOT IT.

PEOPLE! PEOPLE! PLEASE!

IS THIS ANY EXAMPLE TO SET FOR THE TEMPS?

HELEN CAN'T FIGURE IT OUT.

HELEN CAN'T FIGURE IT OUT.

HELEN CAN'T FIGURE IT OUT.

HELEN CAN'T FIGURE IT OUT.

THIS IS INSANE! I'VE CHECKED THE LOGIC BOARDS, BATTERIES, CABLES... FOR GOD'S SAKE, NOTHING IS WRONG!

UH, IT NEEDS TO BE PLUGGED IN.

SURE! BY THE OLD ELECTRICAL STANDARD!

PARANOIA

You want to see something REALLY scary? Turn around from your computer screen sometime and look at the wall you used to stare at before your monitor took its place. You'll see details in paint strokes or lain wallpaper, and you'll know a person was there once in the room where you are now. That is his trail for all time, that wall.

Turn back to the screen and it's changed again! Your old reality is over as if it was never there. In fact, if you think about it, maybe you're not there. Maybe nothing in the world is as you think it is. Maybe swamp rats are flying spaceships and the U.S. Government is in league with Michael Bolton. Maybe Princess Di is alive and Elton John is dead. Maybe Drew Barrymore has talent. It's endless.

From Y2K to corporate power abuse, Helen and her friends run the gamut of techno-fears. Yet underlying all of these nightmares is the one major fear we all feel: that of losing control! For most of us it's the fear of losing control to machines, to the Internet, to the monster of technology. For Helen, however, it's the fear of losing control to her emotions, her compassion, and her vulnerabilities...

HELEN, THERE'S A CHARLES TISDALE FOR YOU ON LINE #2.

HEY, CORKY, WHAT'S UP OLD M.I.T. BUDDY?

OH, LOTS OF STUFF, HELEN. MOST IMPORTANT, I BOUGHT A RANCH.

COOL!

HOW'S THE WORK GOIN' FIXING THE YEAR 2000 BUG?

UHH...

NOT SO GOOD.

GUESS I'D BETTER PANIC, HUH? HEE HEE...

KEEP OUT!

LISTEN, CORKY... THE COMPLEXITY OF THE Y2K PROBLEM IS ALSO ITS SAVING GRACE...

THAT COMPLEXITY WILL DISALLOW ONE MELT DOWN FROM DOMINOING INTO ANOTHER...

IT'S A MESS, CORKY. BUT THE MESS IS WHAT'S GONNA SAVE US, DON'T YOU SEE..? CORKY?

I'M SORRY, HELEN, I WAS COMMUNICATING WITH SPACE ALIENS.

I KNOW THE FEELING.

SOMETHING'S BOTHERING YOU, HELEN. WHAT'S THE MATTER?

AN OLD FRIEND OF MINE FREAKED OUT OVER THE Y2K THING, AND BECAME A SURVIVALIST.

ARE YOU FEELING LIKE MAYBE HE'S GOT A POINT?

WELL, I HAVE TO ADMIT PART OF ME DOES...

BUT THEN I THINK ABOUT IT AND REALIZE I CAN'T POSSIBLY GIVE UP ON THE WORLD!

HOW COME?

WITHOUT ME THE WORLD DOESN'T SURVIVE ANYWAY!

SPENCER, THIS WHOLE Y2K THING REALLY POINTS OUT A PROBLEM WITH HI-TECH PEOPLE...

MY BRILLIANT FRIEND CORKY FREAKS OUT ABOUT IT, AND RUNS OFF TO WAIT FOR THE END OF THE WORLD, RATHER THAN TRY TO FIX THE PROBLEM.

THAT SHOWS A **CRIMINAL** LACK OF SENSITIVITY TO ONE'S FELLOW HUMANS!

YEAH, I GUESS I'VE NOTICED TECHIES ARE LIKE THAT.

OH, YEAH! LIKE YOU WERE **SMART** ENOUGH TO!

HELEN, I NEED YOUR HELP TO GET MY COMPUTER WORKING.

NO.

BUT YOU'RE THE ONLY ONE HERE WHO KNOWS HOW TO RUN THESE THINGS!

YOU'VE GOT A MANUAL, DOUG. USE IT.

I AM!

"ÀSK HELEN!?"

I'M SURE THEY WERE JUST TRYING TO BE EFFICIENT.

YOU KNOW, HELEN, YOU CAN'T BE A TECHIE **ALL** THE TIME.

THAT'S TRUE. MAYBE I SHOULD TRY TO THINK DIFFERENTLY...

HELEN!

THANK GOD YOU DID THAT! MY BRAIN STORPED!

WHAT I WANT TO KNOW, HELEN, IS WHEN ARE WE ALL GONNA BE CYBORGS?

WE ARE NOW!

HEARING AIDS, PACEMAKERS, PROSTHETICS...

CEMENT HEADS.

REALLY?! WHO?

SPENCER, DO WE HAVE A FUTURE?

THAT DEPENDS IF THE YEAR 2000 BUG MAKES THE RUSSIANS ACCIDENTALLY LAUNCH ALL THEIR MISSILES.

I DIDN'T MEAN **THE WORLD**, I MEANT **US!**

OH.

SO YOU THINK I SHOULD CALL YELTSIN BACK?

HELEN, THERE'S A LAW OFFICER HERE TO SEE YOU.

HUH?

MS. NICHOLS? HELEN NICHOLS?

YES.

YOU'RE UNDER ARREST! FOR ILLEGALLY DOWNLOADING MP3 MUSIC FILES OFF THE WORLD WIDE WEB!

BUT WAIT! I DIDN'T THINK THAT APPLIED TO **BOBBY VINTON** MUSIC!

ARE YOU KIDDIING, LADY? FOR THAT YOU SHOULD GET THE **CHAIR!**

WHAT DO YOU MEAN YOU WON'T LET HELEN OUT OF JAIL?

SORRY, SIR. THE JUDGE HAS ISSUED A NO BAIL ORDER.

BUT WHY?

BECAUSE THE JUDGE BELIEVES COMPUTER HACKERS ARE BY NATURE UNREPENTANT SCOFFLAWS!

BUT THAT'S LUDICROUS! HELEN NICHOLS IS AS PRISTINE AND SWEET AS ANY WOMAN YOU'LL EVER MEET!

WHY CYANIDE OF COURSE! ON A TINY NEEDLE INSIDE A PINKY RING.

WOW! I NEVER THINK OF STUFF LIKE THAT!

YOU'RE AN INTERNET MUSIC PIRATE, HELEN?

IT'S A MISUNDER-STANDING, PHIL...

BUT SINCE THE RECORD COMPANIES ARE SO BENT OUT OF SHAPE OVER ON-LINE MUSIC PIRACY, THEY DON'T WANT TO LISTEN!

LOOK, HELEN, I MAY'VE SOLVED OUR PROBLEM...

I HACKED INTO THE PRISON SYSTEM AND HAD YOUR STATUS CHANGED! THEY SHOULD BE HERE ANY MINUTE TO LET YOU OUT.

IT'S TIME TO GO, MY CHILD.

SEE?

UH...

BIBLE

OKAY, NICHOLS, YOU'RE BEIN' RELEASED!

WHA- YOU'RE KIDDING!

NOPE! HERE'S YOUR BENEFACTOR!

BOBBY VINTON!

SIGH.. OH, MR. VINTON, I'M SO SORRY I ILLEGALLY DOWN-LOADED AND PROPAGATED YOUR MUSIC...

I PROMISE I WILL NEVER DO IT AGAIN!

OH, YEAH? BACK IN THE SLAMMER!

HEY, WORK FRIENDS... WHY AREN'T YOU ENJOYING THE PARTY?

"BABYLON 5" IS ON!

OH.

YOU KNOW, THERE ARE A LOT OF BORED, SINGLE WOMEN HERE!

THEY DON'T WANNA WATCH THE "HOME SHOPPING" CHANNEL, DO THEY?!

YOU WANT A RAISE, HELEN?

MMM-HMM. $5,000.00 A YEAR.

YOU DON'T REALLY NEED IT THOUGH, DO YOU?

NAH. I DON'T NEED WHAT I'M MAKING NOW.

YOU KNOW... I COULD SAVE A LOT OF MONEY IF YOU GOT SOME THERAPY TO QUELL YOUR NEED TO THROW WEIGHT AROUND WHENEVER YOU'RE PERSONAL LIFE DISSATISFIES YOU.

GOOD IDEA.

THROW IN ANOTHER $5,000.00 MEDICAL.

SHUT-UP, PHIL.

SO, HELEN, DO YOU WANT TO GIVE US A SYSTEMS ADMINISTRATION REPORT?

SURE, BUT YOU COULDN'T UNDERSTAND IT.

EXCUSE ME? WE'RE DOING SOME THINGS WITH MAINFRAMES AND CLIENT-SERVER TECHNOLOGY, BUT THE DETAILS ARE COMPLETELY LOST ON YOU, SO LET'S JUST DISPENSE WITH THE CHARADE, SHALL WE?

UM, ALL RIGHT.

I WAS WORRIED THERE FOR A SECOND!

I GOT YOU A NEW VERSION OF "MYST."

89

YOU KNOW, WHEN WE DATED FOR REAL AND NOT JUST ON E-MAIL, WE ALWAYS ENDED UP FIGHTING.

YOU ENDED UP FIGHTING. **I** ENDED UP SUFFERING!

YOU KNOW, SUFFERING CAN BE A FORM OF AGGRESSION.

THAT'S LIKE SAYING THE GROIN DAMAGES THE KNEE THAT SMASHES IT!

YOU KNOW SOMETIMES I REALLY MISS OUR PHYSICAL—

BYE!

HIGH TECH. SURE HAS MADE A LOT OF MILLIONAIRES!

AH, WHO NEEDS ALL THAT MONEY?

EXCUSE ME!

YOU CAN LIVE ON A LOT LESS IF YOU WORK AT IT.

FOR EXAMPLE, I PAID ALL MY BILLS LAST MONTH WITH $150.00!

THAT'S 'CAUSE YOU HACKED INTO THE FED AND MADE EACH OF YOUR DOLLARS WORTH 6,000 CENTS!

I WAS CORRECTING INFLATION!

WE'RE SHORT OF MANPOWER. WE HAVE TO RECRUIT SOME NEW WEB PROFESSIONALS.

OKAY...

OFFER $100,000.00 A YEAR AND THEY'LL COME.

WE CAN'T AFFORD THAT!

TAP TAP TAP TAP TAP TAP...

CAN NOW. OUR STOCK PRICE JUST HIT 81!

HELEN, STAY OUT OF NASDAQ!

DID YOU SEE THE MOVIE "THE MATRIX?"

YEAH. BORING.

YOU'RE KIDDING!

COME ON! IT'S AN EMPTY VESSEL SURROUNDED BY BELLS AND WHISTLES ENOUGH TO SEPARATE SUCKERS FROM THEIR MONEY!

BUT THAT'S OUR WHOLE BUSINESS.

WHAT'S THE MATTER, HELEN?

TOO MANY LATE NIGHTS...

TOO MANY TECHNOLOGIES, TOO MANY COMPANIES, TOO MANY DECISIONS...

SIGH...

672,715 DOTS IN THE CEILING.

YOU SAVANTS ARE SCARY.

YOU'RE REALLY DOWN ON TECHIES, AREN'T YOU, HELEN?

NOT AT ALL. I'M A TOTAL TECHIE.

I JUST DON'T LIKE IT WHEN THEY DO THINGS THEY'RE NOT QUALIFIED FOR...

LIKE GO INTO BUSINESS, RAISE FAMILIES, MAKE LIVES...

ANONYMOUS INTIMACY

Intimacy with someone is easy. The hard part is figuring out whether you're gonna buy chunky or smooth.

As the comedy troupe Firesign Theater once put it: "We're all bozos on this bus." On the big city bus that is the Internet, we all tend to be clowns, charming and cajoling each other, and of course trying to get close. The latter is easy because the Internet is so safe and so immediate, safer than a phone and more immediate than going to the neighbors.

Anonymous intimacy is what Helen experiences in all her relationships, with her coworkers as she polices their own intimate e-mails, her bosses as she unwillingly uncovers their secret business and personal desires, and finally herself as she dates the one man she despised above all others.

Hell, would you want to stick around for all that?

We should be very careful not to mistake this for real human closeness. Why? Because on the Greyhound bus that is the Internet — like any bus — the object is and always has been to get off.

LUCY, DO YOU THINK E-MAIL RELATIONSHIPS CAN WORK?

YOU MEAN E-MAIL-ONLY RELATIONSHIPS?

UH-HUH. COMPLETELY VIRTUAL.

HMM...

WELL, I GUESS THERE ARE WAYS TO CHECK...

FOR INSTANCE, HOW DID YOU DO WITH YOUR VIRTUAL PET?

NOT SO GOOD. MY TAMAGACHI GOT RABIES.

WHAT ARE YOU LOOKING AT THIS TIME, LUCY?

IT'S A ROMANCE CHAT ROOM FOR GEEKS.

WE PLAY GAMES WITH EACH OTHER, USE FAKE NAMES AND TRY TO SWEEP EACH OTHER OFF OUR FEET!

"OH, REGGIE, REGGIE... YOU TALL, DARK HANDSOME INDIVIDUAL..."

TAP TAP...

"OH, SHEILA. YOU BIG THING WITH NON-MALE THINGS."

AS I SAY, IT'S FOR GEEKS.

IF I'M GOING TO EXPERIMENT WITH THIS ROMANCE CHAT ROOM, I HAVE TO THINK OF A FAKE NAME...

"HELLO. I'M BILL GATES_"

NO, I CAN'T USE THAT!

TAP TAP...

"HELLO. I'M BILL GATES' SISTER_"

TAP TAP...

"HEY, SIS. WHAT'S UP?"

AAAAAAAAAHH!

JOHN, DOUG TOLD ME HE'D CONVINCED YOU TO USE BULK E-MAIL AS A MARKETING TOOL.

YES! ISN'T IT EXCITING?

NO! IT'S **AWFUL**! IT'S ABSOLUTELY AGAINST **NETIQUETTE**!

"NETIQUETTE!" ISN'T THAT ANOTHER ONE OF THOSE **COOL INTERNET TERMS**?

SIGH... YES.

"NETIQUETTE," "SPAMMING..." I WANT TO DO **ALL THE COOL** TERMS! I WANT TO BE IN THE **FRONT FOUR** OF TECHNOLOGY!

THAT'S **FOREFRONT** OF TECHNOLOGY.

HELL! IT COULD BE **FOUR ON THE FLOOR** OF TECHNOLOGY! WE'LL MAKE UP OUR **OWN** TERMS!

JOHN REFUSES TO QUIT BULK E-MAILING, SO I'M FORCED TO DO A WORKAROUND.

A "WORKAROUND?"

I'M MAKING A "BOT" THAT'LL CAUSE ANY ATTEMPT AT BULK E-MAILING TO SELF-DESTRUCT.

BUT AREN'T YOU GOING AGAINST COMPANY POLICY?

PHIL, I **AM** COMPANY POLICY.

ALL RIGHT. WHY DON'T WE HAVE A BETTER HEALTH PLAN?

'CAUSE I DON'T HAVE TIME TO HACK BLUE CROSS.

DAD BLAST IT! MY HOME PHONE'S STILL BUSY 'CAUSE MY DAUGHTER'S ON AOL!

WHY DON'T YOU GIVE HER HER OWN PHONE!

SHE'S ONLY 13.

PHIL, WHEN I WAS 13 I RAN AN ENTIRE I.T. DEPARTMENT!

YOU'RE DIFFERENT.

HOW AM I DIFFERENT?

I CAN'T CONTROL YOU.

WHICH IS WHY YOU'RE MY BOSS!

NOT THAT YOU CAN EVER QUOTE ME AS CARING, BUT IF YOU AND DOUG ARE GONNA DATE, WHAT ABOUT SPENCER?

WELL...

SPENCER AND I AREN'T INVOLVED. HE SAID SO.

STILL, YOU HAVE FEELINGS FOR HIM, DON'T YOU?

YES, YES, I DO.

BUT THEN, I ALSO HAVE FEELINGS FOR THE **MAC PLUS.**

HELLO, DOUG.

HELEN! WHAT ARE YOU DOING HERE!?

I HAD A CHANGE OF HEART ABOUT OUR RELATIONSHIP. I WANT TO TALK.

SUPPOSE I DON'T **WANT** TO TALK!

≥SMACK!≤

HERE'S MY OFFER...

GOD, I LOVE DEMOS!

THE WHOLE IDEA OF DATING IS RIDICULOUSLY OUTMODED...

SO WHAT I PROPOSE FOR US IS A MAINTENENCE PROCEDURE... A WEEKLY INSPECTION AND RETOOLING OF PRIMARY SENSORY PORTS...

WHAT DO YOU THINK?

ANY UPLOADING?

IF YOU'RE SWEET.

I KNOW I'VE ANTAGONIZED YOU IN THE PAST, DOUG, BUT I'VE DECIDED TO TURN OVER A NEW LEAF...

SO YOU CAN BE YOUR BIG **MALE SELF** AND NOT WORRY THAT I'M GOING TO REACT IN ANY SCARY **RETALIATORY** FASHION.

YOU'RE BEING FRESH RIGHT AWAY THEN?

NO, I'M CHECKING FOR A WIRE.

I CAN'T BELIEVE YOU, HELEN! YOU'VE COMPLETELY CHANGED!

YOU'RE YIELDING AND NON-ASSERTIVE! YOU HAVEN'T MADE A DECISION **ALL NIGHT!**

I EXPECTED A CHALLENGING, PROVOKING WOMAN, AND TO MY PLEASANT SURPRISE, WHAT DID I GET?

A TOTAL MORON!

WELL, I WANT US TO WORK, DOUG...

GOD, I HAVEN'T DANCED IN AGES!

I DIDN'T THINK YOU COULD.

OH? AND WHY NOT?

YOU'RE A GEEK! I THOUGHT YOU WERE AFRAID OF ANYTHING PHYSICAL!

C-CAN I GO WATCH "STAR TREK," NOW?

103

107

THE SUPERSTAR

Long ago a young boy named Bill Gates was born and raised in a family not too dissimilar from yours. He grew up, went to school, got into scrapes, dealt with cops, partied, etc. He was a guy.

Then he became the richest man in the entire, known and unknown, considered, or ever even imagined, universe.

If you thought Helen was an amazing freak of nature, meet Bill. He climbs skyscrapers, fights grizzly bears, and boxes rounds with Lenox Lewis. He brushes his teeth with gold and scents himself with the dust of his enemies. He is Pharaoh MSN I, and he holds court with scepter and crown... Until Moses comes along in the form of the Department of Justice to inform him that his ledger of black ink will be parted in the near future...

HELLO. THIS IS HELEN.

HELEN, I'M BOB HARKIN. HUMAN RESOURCES STAFF AT MICROSOFT.

MICROSOFT? WHY ARE YOU GUYS COURTING ME?

ARE YOU KIDDING? YOU'RE ONE OF THE BEST CODERS THAT EVER LIVED!

YEAH, BUT I'M OUT OF CODING, BOB. I'M WAY TOO OLD.

AT 24?

58 IN TECHNO-STRESS YEARS.

SO? WE'RE NOT "AGEIST."

BOB, I'M REALLY NOT INTERESTED IN CHANGING JOBS.

BUT THIS IS **MICROSOFT** CALLING!

YEAH, SO? YOU MAKE MEDIOCRE SOFTWARE AND BLUDGEON PEOPLE TO DEATH WITH YOUR MARKETING DOLLARS. BIG DEAL!

WHO TOLD YOU THAT?

BILL GATES! HE TRIED TO RECRUIT ME SOME YEARS BACK AT THE PC WORLD EXPO.

BILL TRIED TO RECRUIT YOU?

WELL, MAYBE "RECRUIT" ISN'T QUITE THE RIGHT WORD...

COME ON, HELEN... COME OUT TO SEATTLE, AND SEE WHAT MICROSOFT'S ABOUT BEFORE YOU SAY NO TO US.

YOU'RE WASTING YOUR TIME, BOB.

LOOK, HELEN... I DON'T WANT TO PLAY ROUGH, BUT WE **REALLY REALLY** WANT YOU TO RECONSIDER.

WHAT DO YOU MEAN "PLAY ROUGH?"

HELEN, DID YOU HEAR? MICROSOFT'S MAKING A HOSTILE BID TO BUY OUR COMPANY!

SO, 2:00 PM, TUESDAY?

HELEN, THE WORLD OF INFORMATION SYSTEMS IS A TOWER OF BABEL OF COMPETING STANDARDS...

AT MICROSOFT WE WILL CHANGE ALL THAT. WITH YOUR HELP, WE CAN UNITE THE WORLD UNDER ONE STANDARD, ONE LANGUAGE.

AND RULE THE GALAXY TOGETHER!

BILL, HAVE YOU BEEN DIGITALLY ENHANCED?

WELL, IF NO IS YOUR FINAL ANSWER...

I'M AFRAID IT IS.

YOU KNOW, OF COURSE, MICROSOFT IS GOING TO TAKE OVER THE WORLD.

THEN I'LL BE A LITTLE MAMMAL RUNNING BETWEEN THE DINOSAUR'S LEGS.

DINOSAUR, EH? YOU IMPLY OUR EXTINCTION?

NO. JUST YOUR MASSIVE COLD-BLOODEDNESS.

OH! NO BIG DEAL THEN!

RIGHT.

YOU TOLD BILL GATES TO GO SUCK EGGS?

IN SO MANY WORDS, YES.

JEEZ, IS HE GONNA LET YOU LIVE?

CAREER-WISE, WHO KNOWS? HE CERTAINLY IS POWERFUL.

I'VE ALWAYS WONDERED... IS HE REALLY LIKE ROSS PEROT?

YES, BUT WITH MONEY.

PHIL, HAVE YOU SEEN, HELEN?

SHE TOOK THE DAY OFF TO CLEAN HER HOUSE.

WHY DOESN'T SHE JUST **HIRE** SOMEONE? WHO'S SHE TRYING TO IMPRESS?

I'M ASKING MYSELF THE SAME QUESTION ABOUT BILL GATES...

WHY IN THE WORLD IS HE BAILING OUT APPLE? WHO IS HE TRYING TO IMPRESS?

TA DA!

OH, NO.

BILL GATES, **WHAT** ARE YOU DOING?

SAVING THE WORLD! MAY I COME IN?

SO TELL ME, BLONDIE... DID MY SLAYING OF APPLE'S DRAGONS IMPRESS YOU?

KNOCK IT OFF! IT'S THE ANTITRUST FOLKS **YOU** WANT TO IMPRESS.

MAYBE, BUT YOU MUST ADMIT, IT WAS ONE OF THE MOST **CREATIVE** IDEAS ANYONE COULD HAVE!

PLEASE! YOU NEVER HAD A CREATIVE IDEA IN YOUR **LIFE!**

TRICKING IBM OUT OF DOS WASN'T CREATIVE?

FOR **AL CAPONE!**

BLONDIE, YOU'RE WRONG TO THINK I SAVED APPLE SIMPLY TO PUT OFF THE ANTITRUST PEOPLE...

THIS IS ABOUT **PARTNERING!** THIS IS ABOUT BRINGING TO THE WORLD A NEW SPIRIT OF **COOPERATION!**

THIS IS ABOUT DECENT MICROSOFT APPLICATIONS FOR THE MAC! THIS IS ABOUT APPLE PUSHING **INTERNET EXPLORER!**

THIS IS ABOUT YOU DESTROYING **NETSCAPE.**

YESSS!!!

117

TIM BERNERS-LEE SURE WAS A VISIONARY TO COME UP WITH THE WORLD WIDE WEB, WASN'T HE, HELEN?

I THOUGHT OF IT, TOO, YOU KNOW.

OH, **SURE!**

HEY, YOU'VE NEVER HEARD OF SYNCHRONICITY?

TIM AND I BOTH HAD THE SAME IDEA AT THE SAME TIME. HE JUST HAD BETTER LUCK.

HE CALLED "HEADS."

WHAT'S THAT?

HELEN'S I.D. FROM M.I.T.

"HELEN ARIANA NICHOLS, AGE 14." WOW, SHE REALLY **WAS** A PRODIGY!

HERE'S A SERIES OF I.D.S FOR THE VARIOUS FIRMS SHE WORKED FOR.

LOOK! HERE'S A RESIGNATION NOTE TO APPLE.

AND A NOTE SHE GOT BACK...

"WHO'S AN ARROGANT JERK? SEE YOU IN HELL!" -STEVE JOBS.

WOW. THEY SOUND LIKE GOOD FRIENDS!

BUT SERIOUSLY, HELEN... AREN'T YOU AT LEAST A **LITTLE** CONCERNED YOUR LOVE OF COMPUTERS MAKES YOU SEEM UNFEMININE?

TO WHOM, GWEN?

TO MORONIC **MAMA'S BOYS** WHO NEVER GOT BEYOND PLAYBOY MAGAZINE?!

WHAT ELSE IS THERE?

BILL GATES?

EEWW!

HERE'S YOUR TEA.

THANK YOU.

OH. LIPTON.

I'M SORRY IT'S NOT IMPORTED. IT'S ALL I HAVE IN THE HOUSE.

THAT'S OKAY.

I THINK I OWN THEM.

SIGH...

THE JUDGE CALLING ME A MONOPOLIST AND AN UNFAIR BUSINESSMAN DESTROYED ME, HELEN...

ALL MY LIFE I'VE BEEN THE GOLDEN BOY. SAFE. UNSULLIED...

NOW, I'VE BEEN TARNISHED! I'M NO LONGER GOLDEN! I'M NOT PERFECT!

HELEN, I COULD CONCEIVABLY DIE SOMEDAY!

KEEP HOLDING MY HAND, DUDE, AND YOU CAN COUNT ON IT!

SIGH... GOOD-BYE.

WHO'S THAT?

JUST A GUY I KNOW..

OH.

YOU OKAY?

YEAH.

WAIT... WAS THAT STEVE JOBS?

MAYBE SOME DAY.